BENJAMIN O. DAVIS JR.

BENJAMIN O. DAVIS JR.

AIR FORCE GENERAL & TUSKEGEE AIRMEN LEADER

by Sari Earl

Content Consultant:
Randy J. Garibay LTC (Ret), USA
African & African American Studies Instructor, University of Oklahoma

ABDO
Publishing Company

CREDITS

Published by ABDO Publishing Company, 8000 West 78th Street, Edina, Minnesota 55439. Copyright © 2010 by Abdo Consulting Group, Inc. International copyrights reserved in all countries. No part of this book may be reproduced in any form without written permission from the publisher. The Essential Library™ is a trademark and logo of ABDO Publishing Company.

Printed in the United States of America,
North Mankato, Minnesota
102009
012010

 PRINTED ON RECYCLED PAPER

Editor: Mari Kesselring
Copy Editor: Paula Lewis
Interior Design and Production: Kazuko Collins
Cover Design: Kazuko Collins

Library of Congress Cataloging-in-Publication Data
Earl, Sari.
  Benjamin O. Davis, Jr. : Air Force general & Tuskegee Airmen leader / Sari Earl.
    p. cm. — (Military heroes)
  Includes bibliographical references.
  ISBN 978-1-60453-961-5
  1. Davis, Benjamin O. (Benjamin Oliver), 1912—Juvenile literature. 2. Generals—United States—Biography—Juvenile literature. 3. African American generals—Biography—Juvenile literature. 4. United States. Air Force—Biography—Juvenile literature. I. Title.

  UG626.2.D37E375 2010
  358.40092—dc22
  [B]
                                        2009032339

Benjamin O. Davis, Jr.

TABLE OF CONTENTS

Chapter 1

Ben went to see a barnstorming event in 1926.

Flying High
in the Wind

An airplane swooped high above the clouds in Washington DC. Benjamin O. Davis Jr. was only 13 years old as he stood at Bolling Field watching pilots in airplanes entertain the crowd with clever tricks. Ben's Uncle Ernest had read about the barnstorming event in the newspaper. Although Uncle Ernest had no real interest in airplanes, he thought his nephew might enjoy the show. Little did Ernest know that the trip would spark a lifelong interest in aviation for Ben. Ben was mesmerized by the sight of the airplanes. For the rest of his life, he would remember that blue sky and the airplanes that danced across it.

Uncle Ernest

Uncle Ernest was Ben's mother's brother. He was one of Ben's favorite uncles. Uncle Ernest often took his nephew on special trips such as going to the barnstorming event, visiting relatives, and taking streetcar rides in the city. Ben remembered these trips fondly even many years later. He also remembered that Uncle Ernest often gave him spending money.

After Ben and his uncle returned home from Bolling Field, Ben told his father, Benjamin O. Davis Sr., all about the exciting event. Davis Sr. decided to take Ben back to see the airplanes again. This time Ben was going to get a ride in one of the airplanes.

FIRST RIDE

When Ben and his father arrived at Bolling Field's dirt runway, Ben was barely able to contain his anticipation. He could not quite believe that his father was going to spend five dollars so that he could go up in an airplane. That was a lot to spend in 1926, and Ben's father was always careful with his money. Yet there he stood, ready to pay for Ben to get a chance to soar in the sky. As young Ben waited, he tried to stand straight and not fidget with excitement. His father was a military man who expected Ben to keep himself composed in public.

Only a short time later, Ben climbed into the open cockpit. The airplane looked fragile to Ben, and he wondered if it was going to be able to carry him and the pilot. He put on goggles and a helmet as the pilot directed. When

Barnstorming

After World War I, pilots and airplanes were in greater supply because of wartime training programs. The army sold airplanes that had been used in the war at reduced prices. Many former World War I pilots purchased these planes and used them to entertain crowds.

The pilots who flew the airplanes and performed stunts were called barnstormers. A new phase in aviation began in the 1920s, as barnstorming became popular. The barnstormers typically would find an open field on a farm and get permission from the owner to use the area for landings. The pilot then would advertise the event. In many rural towns, when a barnstormer arrived, people dropped what they were doing to catch the show. Many would enjoy the spectacle, while some brave souls would pay for a ride in an airplane.

Although entertaining, barnstorming was dangerous for both the crowd and the performers. The airplanes bought after the war were not always safe, and many of the stunts were dangerous. Many barnstormers died in crashes. One risky stunt involved performers called wing walkers. Wing walkers would walk along an airplane's wing while it was in flight. Some of them would even jump from the wing of one plane to the wing of another.

the airplane finally took off, Ben was filled with exhilaration. The airplane swooped high into the white clouds.

After a few moments, Ben looked down. The city of Washington DC was spread out before him. Suddenly, he was filled with determination to become an aviator.

BEN'S DREAM

Ben's resolve to become an aviator was only enhanced when Charles Lindbergh flew solo across the Atlantic Ocean to Paris a year later in 1927. Lindbergh became a national celebrity because of the groundbreaking trip. Ben was obsessed with the flight and read everything he could about the aviator.

Unfortunately for Ben, in the 1920s, there were no means by which an African-American man could become a professional pilot. Typically, career opportunities for African Americans were restricted. Those with limited education took

Air Mail

When Ben was young, airplanes were just starting to be used in many new ways. One new way that airplanes were used in the 1920s was to help deliver mail. Mail delivered by air was called "Air Mail." On February 2, 1925, a new law allowed the U.S. Post Office to contract with private air carriers to deliver mail.

Benjamin O. Davis Sr.

the service jobs that many white people did not want. Many African Americans became waiters, street cleaners, and elevator operators. Some African-American men, if they had the required education, could become doctors, ministers, and lawyers. But even in these professions, they were often confined in their occupations by not being allowed to work with white people.

DETERMINATION

Growing up, Benjamin O. Davis Jr. had a good education. His family had made sure of that. But he was not interested in becoming a minister or a doctor. Ben believed in his dream, regardless of not immediately seeing a realistic way to become an aviator.

That determination, mixed with his father's influence as a role model, would propel Ben to pursue a military career. As a young man Ben decided that, no matter what the obstacles before him, he would attend the United States Military Academy at West Point in New York. He was well aware of the hurdles he would face. His father had wanted to go to West Point, but racism had closed that route to him. As an officer, his father also regularly faced discrimination in the army. The U.S. War Department made every effort to avoid assignments for Davis Sr. where he might command white enlisted men or outrank a white officer. Thus, his career was hampered by "safe" assignments. Ben Jr. would face some of those

West Point

The United States Military Academy at West Point is located in southern New York. The site of West Point has been occupied continuously by troops since 1778. It is the oldest active military post in the United States. Congress established the United States Military Academy at West Point in 1802. The academy opened on July 4 of that year. At that time, it was primarily a school for military engineers. In 1812, an act of Congress restructured the academy, enlarged the student body, and made it a four-year college.

What Is Segregation?

Segregation is the separation or isolation of a race, class, or ethnic group. This policy makes the minority group second-class citizens. It also promotes the interests of the ruling class by providing its members with the best facilities and employment and educational opportunities.

In the 1870s, the Southern state legislatures passed laws requiring the separation of whites from "persons of color" in public transportation and schools. These laws were known as Jim Crow laws. These laws helped whites enforce racial segregation in the South from the late nineteenth century into the beginning of the civil rights movement in the 1950s.

same conflicts in his military career. However, in Ben's generation, things were slowly starting to change in the United States for African Americans. People were fighting back against racism. They were questioning the value of segregation policies that kept whites and blacks apart. The situation was changing in the military, too.

Benjamin O. Davis Jr.'s commitment to the United States and his determination to become an aviator would help transform the U.S. military forever. He would join the military at a pivotal point in history. He would be part of many critical changes in the armed forces, some of which he was instrumental in bringing about. The 13-year-old boy flying above Bolling Field on that sunny day in 1926 had no idea how high he would one day fly.

Benjamin O. Davis Jr. was determined to become a pilot.

Benjamin O. Davis Sr. was ordered to teach at Wilberforce University, an African-American institution.

A CHILD OF THE MILITARY

enjamin O. Davis Jr. was born on December 18, 1912, in his grandfather's home in Washington DC. His mother was Elnora Dickerson Davis, a dressmaker from a large family of seven girls and two boys. Ben's father, Benjamin O.

Davis Sr., was the youngest of three children. At the time of Ben's birth, his father was a first lieutenant of cavalry at Fort D. A. Russell, Wyoming, and the couple already had one child.

Benjamin O. Davis Sr. was a committed military man who had tried to get into West Point. But he was told that, for political reasons, African Americans could not be appointed to the military academy. So, Davis Sr. pursued his military career by enlisting in the army.

Before Ben was born, his father had been stationed at various posts, including Fort Washakie, Wyoming; Fort Robinson, Nebraska; and Wilberforce, Ohio. After Ben was born, the traveling continued. Ben's father was stationed on the Mexican border from 1912 to 1915, during the Mexican Revolution. If the conditions were deemed safe, Elnora and the children joined Benjamin O. Davis Sr. where he was stationed.

In February 1915, Davis Sr. was ordered once more to Wilberforce University, an African-American institution where he had taught from 1905 to 1909. He was stationed there to teach military science and tactics despite his strong preference for duty with troops. But the U.S. War

Department intentionally ordered Davis Sr. to assignments where he would not be in command of white enlisted men or outrank a white officer. This kind of racist policy significantly impacted his career.

Benjamin O. Davis Sr.

Benjamin O. Davis Sr. was born in 1877 in Washington DC. His mother was a nurse and his father worked for the federal government. Davis volunteered to serve in the U.S. Army in the Spanish-American War of 1898. His parents did not approve of his chosen career path. His father viewed enlisted men as being low in status and pay. His mother would have preferred that her son become a minister. In Washington, he had been known as Ollie Davis, but he enlisted as Benjamin O. Davis.

Upon joining the army, Davis realized that he had an advantage over most of his fellow servicemen since he could both read and write. Davis rose to the highest enlisted rank in the army—sergeant major. Thereafter, he passed his examinations and became an officer in 1901. He continued his military career with postings including, but not limited to, the Philippines, Liberia, and along the U.S.-Mexico border. In 1938, he took command of the 369th Cavalry of the New York National Guard. This was a regiment of African-American troops. Davis was later promoted to the rank of brigadier general. He was the first African-American general in the U.S. Army.

A BIG FAMILY

On February 9, 1916, while living at Wilberforce, the Davis family welcomed a new member, Elnora Jr. Ben's mother died suddenly soon after the baby's birth. Davis Sr. was left alone to care for his children while pursuing a military career that required travel. A number of family members offered to take one of the children. But

only Ben's grandmother, Henrietta
Davis, was willing to take all three.
Ben's father wanted to keep his
children together. So in May 1917,
he moved his children to Washington
DC to live with his parents, Louis and
Henrietta Davis. Shortly thereafter,
Davis Sr. left for an assignment in the
Philippines, a tour of duty expected
to last two years.

Washington DC

In 1800, Washington DC
became the capital of the
United States of America.
The city was named after
George Washington and
Christopher Columbus.
(DC stands for "District
of Columbia.") Situated
between Virginia and
Maryland, the city is often
referred to as DC or the
District.

That two-year tour stretched to three years.
During that time, Ben and his sisters continued to
stay in Washington DC with their father's family.
Their mother's family lived close by and was a strong
presence in their lives. Ben enjoyed his uncles and
aunts. His Uncle Ernest helped him get his first job
as a paperboy for the *Evening Star*. When Ben was old
enough, he attended a neighborhood school for
African Americans. All the teachers and the students
were African Americans, and the school provided an
excellent education.

Ben's younger years were very positive.
He enjoyed his big extended family and his
neighborhood. One negative aspect, however, was
the race riots that occurred not far from Ben's home

when he was still young. Although the riots never directly touched him, Ben always remembered the fear he heard in the voices of the adults in his family. He never forgot the warnings to stay away from certain streets near their home. Those events were Ben's first memories of racial issues.

Meanwhile, still stationed in the Philippines, Ben's father wrote letters to Sadie Overton. She was a professor of English that he knew from Wilberforce. Sadie came from a family where education was highly valued. Davis Sr. courted Sadie by mail. Sadie went to the Philippines in 1919 and married Davis Sr. on December 24. Mother Sadie, as Ben called her, became a positive influence on Ben.

TUSKEGEE INSTITUTE

In 1920, Davis Sr. was transferred to Alabama's historically African-American Tuskegee Institute to teach. Again, discrimination may have been behind this assignment. Davis Sr. was kept away from troops and from lower ranking white officers.

The family moved to Tuskegee Institute and lived in a bungalow close to the Lincoln Gates, the entrance to campus. The children adjusted easily to Mother Sadie, who took a keen interest in their education. The house was disciplined. The children were expected to do well in school and to be obedient, neat, and punctual.

Ben attended Children's House, a private elementary school for inhabitants of the Tuskegee Institute. Ben did well in school and enjoyed his classes. He did take issue, however, with his piano lessons. He did not like his piano instructor and resented learning traditional, instead of modern, music. Eventually, he stopped playing the piano, a decision he would later regret.

One incident in Tuskegee remained forever etched in Ben's mind—witnessing a Ku Klux Klan march. Not far from the Tuskegee Institute, a new hospital for African-American veterans was being built. The hospital was going to hire African-American doctors and nurses. Apparently, the Ku Klux Klan opposed the fact that jobs would

Tuskegee Institute

In 1881, Booker T. Washington founded Tuskegee Institute to train teachers and teach trade and agricultural skills. He knew that learning these skills would help African Americans become self-reliant. Washington served as principal until he died in 1915.

In the 1920s, Tuskegee shifted focus. It became a college of many fields. In 1943, the Tuskegee Institute began offering graduate-level courses as well. In 1985, it became a full-fledged university.

Ku Klux Klan

During the 1920s, the Ku Klux Klan was an active organization that tried to promote white supremacy through intimidation and violence. The organization targeted African Americans, Jews, members of other minority groups, and foreigners.

The Klan was considered the primary instigator of violence against African Americans in the South. The Klansmen wore white robes and paraded through streets. They burned crosses in neighborhoods at night. The organization aimed to invoke terror in the minds of its targets. For a variety of reasons, including community leaders' rejection of the Klan, support for the group declined rapidly after 1925.

not be going to white doctors and nurses. Klan members marched through the institute in protest.

All the families at the institute had official orders to turn off their lights and remain indoors so as not to provoke the marchers. But Davis Sr. would not cower in the shadows. As a regular army officer, Benjamin O. Davis Sr. donned his white dress uniform. He, his wife, and his three children sat quietly on their porch as the Ku Klux Klan marched by. Ben was ten or eleven years old at the time. His father's actions indicated that his family wanted others to respect them.

*The Davis family lived just outside the
Tuskegee Institute's Lincoln Gates.*

Ben wanted to attend the United States Military Academy at West Point.

SILENCE IS DEAFENING

*I*n the summer of 1924, the army assigned Davis Sr. to Cleveland, Ohio. He moved his family from Tuskegee into a Cleveland neighborhood and Ben attended Cleveland Central High School. The students were African American,

white, Italian, Polish, and other nationalities, and
there were African-American and white teachers.
Ben's grades placed him at the very top of his class.
He was elected president of the student council.
In 1929, Ben graduated and enrolled in Western
Reserve University at Cleveland. He was 16 years old.

Ben still dreamed of becoming an aviator.
However, there were still no paths available to an
African-American man to become a professional
pilot. He was a math major at Western Reserve
University and considered becoming an engineer.
But his heart was not in his study, and he was
frustrated.

But in July 1929, an event at West Point gave
Ben hope. Alonzo Parham, an African-American
man from Chicago, entered West Point. He had
been appointed to the military academy by Oscar
De Priest, an African-American representative in
Congress. De Priest was especially concerned about
rights for African Americans. He often used his
position as congressman to combat racism.

Ben and his family followed the news of Alonzo
Parham very closely. Then, Parham was discharged
from West Point in December 1929 due to academic
deficiency. It was not uncommon for students, even

white students, to be discharged during their first year at West Point. In fact, one-third of the first-year class was discharged. Still, the event prompted Ben's father to write to Congressman De Priest. Davis Sr. expressed his hopes that Parham might reenter West Point since cadets were allowed to retake examinations. De Priest and Davis Sr. also exchanged letters on the subject of African Americans in the military.

Oscar De Priest

Oscar De Priest was born in Florence, Alabama, in 1871 to former slaves. In the 1880s, De Priest moved to Chicago, where he worked as a painter and developed an interest in community issues. De Priest soon discovered that he had a talent for politics. Starting in 1904, he served two terms as Cook County commissioner. He also became very successful as a real estate agent during this time. In 1915, he was voted alderman of the Second Ward in Chicago. This made him Chicago's first African American elected to city council. After two years, he resigned from the office when he was charged for accepting money from a gambling organization. He was later found not guilty of the charges. He ran for reelection in 1918 but lost.

In 1928, De Priest became famous for winning a seat in the U.S. House of Representatives. He was the first African American from a northern state to achieve this honor. Working to increase the rights of African Americans, De Priest became somewhat of a spokesman for all African Americans in the country, including Benjamin O. Davis Jr.

Entering West Point

Ben's path became clear to him. Regardless of the obstacles, he would attend the United States Military Academy at

West Point and pursue a military career. In a letter to De Priest, Davis Sr. suggested his son as a candidate for West Point.

Congressman De Priest offered Ben an appointment to West Point in 1930. However, as a congressman for Illinois, De Priest could only appoint people who lived in Illinois. Ben could not take the appointment because he was not a resident. Ben and his parents decided that Ben should move to Illinois. In the fall of 1930, Ben entered the University of Chicago and became a resident of Illinois.

On February 9, 1931, Ben received his appointment to West Point by De Priest. Ben reported to Fort Sheridan, Illinois, for examinations. He did not realize, however, that he would have to take the academic part of the examination. He had thought that with his one and one-half years of college with good grades he would be exempt from this test. Ben was not prepared for this test, and he was mortified when he failed it. He wrote a letter apologizing to his father and family for letting them down. In his reply, Davis Sr. offered support and expressed his full confidence in his son. His father's words were exactly what Ben needed.

Congressman Oscar De Priest, right, helped Ben get into West Point.

He was even more determined to get into West Point, graduate, and seek a career in the U.S. Army Air Corps.

Ben studied intensely for his next chance at the entrance examination. When he reported to Fort Sheridan in March 1932, he was fully prepared. In early May, Ben received notification from the U.S. War Department that he had passed his examination. He would report to West Point on July 1, 1932.

ISOLATION AT WEST POINT

The military training at West Point is rigorous. Many cadets never graduate. Ben was determined not to be one of those cadets. However, West Point would not be easy for Ben. At first, he assumed that every cadet was exposed to the same treatment as he was. Eventually, he realized that he was receiving treatment that was different from any other cadet.

Ben's first indication of such treatment came when he realized that he had his own room, despite the fact that it was a room designed to house two cadets. It was pointed out to him by the commandant of cadets that no white student would be asked to room with him. Ben felt that this was inconsistent with the principles of West Point—"Duty, Honor, Country." During his four years at West Point, even when the class traveled, Ben would always be assigned his own room.

Ben came to feel isolated at West Point. Later in life, he would clearly recall any kind words he received there—they stood out starkly from the silent treatment he received most often. But instead of making him despair, this treatment fueled Ben's determination to succeed. He did not complain about being isolated. Instead, he held his head high

Encouraging Letters

After his graduation from West Point and throughout his military career, Benjamin O. Davis Jr. received many letters of support and admiration. Several letters of recognition came from some of his former classmates at West Point. Some even contained apologies for the treatment he had received. Others recognized the extra challenges he had been forced to confront at West Point. Davis was glad to receive the letters.

and worked hard. In 1933, Ben received an encouraging letter from Alonzo Parham.

Making it through West Point training was a great source of pride for Ben. He had learned to endure intense physical and emotional hardships. Another highlight during his time at West Point was meeting Agatha Scott at a New Year's Eve party. Agatha was from New Haven, Connecticut. Ben was immediately interested in her. The couple began spending a lot of time together.

During his third year at West Point, Ben undertook tactical training and went to Mitchell Field, where the cadets were introduced to flying. The experience intensified Ben's desire to become a pilot. In October 1935, Ben applied to enter the U.S. Army Air Corps. He was rejected because there were no African-American units in the air corps. Ben was severely disappointed and frustrated. But the rejection made him want to continue to work hard to overcome prejudices and achieve success in the military.

West Point cadets having lunch

Davis graduated from West Point in 1936.

THE TUSKEGEE EXPERIMENT

Benjamin O. Davis Jr. graduated from the United States Military Academy at West Point in June 1936. At graduation, he ranked thirty-fifth in a class of 276. With that class standing, he should have had a choice of great opportunities in any branch of service in the military. Yet, Davis's race still limited his assignments.

After he graduated from West Point, Davis was given a commission as a second lieutenant of infantry. He was to report to the Twenty-fourth Infantry Regiment in Fort Benning, Georgia, on September 12. Before reporting to Fort Benning, Davis married Agatha Scott on June 20 at Cadet Chapel at West Point. After a short break to visit family, Davis traveled with Agatha south to report for duty.

HEADING SOUTH

Traveling south in 1936 held difficulties for the newlyweds. They were restricted to use only "colored" bathrooms and had to stay away from "white-only" establishments. State and local law enforcement took segregation laws very seriously. There were very few rest stops and motels available to them along the road. As many other people of color did at that time, Davis and Agatha made do. They slept in their car on the trip to Georgia.

During the ride, Davis and Agatha studied the rules of protocol for social and military life as a second lieutenant. These written rules had been presented to Davis before graduation from West Point. Davis and Agatha were prepared to be active members of the military base. Upon their arrival, however, they soon discovered that the white officers at Fort Benning were not prepared to include them. When Davis and Agatha tried to follow the rules of etiquette to properly call on commanding officers, they were snubbed. When Davis tried to join the Fort Benning Officers' Club, he was rejected. Davis would later recall, "This was one of the most insulting actions taken against me during my military service."[1] Fort Benning was segregated. It did not matter

Restricted and Insulted

Benjamin O. Davis Jr. and his wife Agatha deeply felt the rejection they experienced when they tried to enter the Fort Benning Officers' Club. Captain Phasey suggested that Davis formally apply for membership to the Fort Benning Officers' Club. Davis immediately filled out an application. He made certain to enclose a check before he mailed the form to the club. Davis and his wife received a response by mail from the club secretary. The secretary wrote that the club had assumed Davis was not interested in being a member, as he had not used the club yet. His check was returned with the letter. It was humiliating to the couple.

Davis believed that Captain Phasey and the club secretary orchestrated events to keep Davis and his wife out of the Fort Benning Officers' Club while making it appear as if they had been offered a chance to join. Davis later stated that this incident was one of the most insulting actions ever taken against him and his wife by the military. In all of his many years of service in the military, Davis never stepped foot into the Fort Benning Officers' Club.

that Davis was a second lieutenant and an esteemed graduate of West Point; the color of his skin dictated how he and his wife were treated.

Despite feeling isolated at Fort Benning, Davis performed his duties well and received excellent reports. Still, Davis wondered if, like his father, he would not be given duties with white troops or units. Most African Americans were restricted to support positions.

BACK TO TUSKEGEE

In March 1938, Davis received orders assigning him to the Tuskegee Institute. Just as his father did, Davis was to teach military science and tactics at the African-American institution. Davis was disappointed. He wanted the military to utilize his talents and provide him with other opportunities. After the move, Davis continued to advance and was promoted to captain of infantry in September 1940. Davis and Agatha enjoyed community activities and friendships at the Tuskegee Institute. Still, they could not ignore the segregation in the town of Tuskegee itself.

In fall of 1940, President Franklin D. Roosevelt nominated Davis's father for promotion to the rank of brigadier general. Benjamin O. Davis Sr. was then assigned to command the Fourth Cavalry Brigade. The brigade was made up of the Ninth and Tenth Cavalry regiments. Most of the men in the regiments were African American. Only officers were white. Davis's father had the power to request his own aides. He requested that his son be reassigned as his aide. The U.S. War Department approved the request, and Davis Jr. and Agatha moved to Fort Riley, Kansas, in 1941.

A New Assignment

Around this time, the Roosevelt administration directed the U.S. War Department to create an African-American flying unit. This was an important step for the U.S. military in 1941. Only a few short weeks after Davis and Agatha arrived in Kansas, Davis's father received a letter from the Office of the U.S. Army Air Corps requesting that his son be released for pilot training. The expectation was that Davis Jr. would complete pilot training and then command an all-African-American flying squadron. Davis Jr. was elated. His dream of becoming an aviator would come true. Davis's father immediately approved his son's reassignment.

Davis reported to the first African-American pilot training class in spring of 1941. It took place at what would later become Tuskegee Army Air Field (TAAF). At the time, the entire "experiment" regarding an African-American fighter squadron was controversial. Some argued that it perpetuated segregation. Others believed that it was a step in the right direction for racial equality. Yet others felt that it would never work because they held racist beliefs that African Americans were inferior.

The people of the town of Tuskegee were hostile toward African Americans and the entire enterprise at TAAF. The town was strictly segregated, and the local law enforcement officers were known to be particularly racist. The citizens of the town wrote letters, signed petitions, and contacted their senators to stop the building of the African-American airfield. The U.S. Army Air Corps moved forward with its plan despite controversy within its own ranks and the grumblings of the citizens of Tuskegee.

Fake Diagnosis

To prepare for pilot training, Davis was ordered to report for a flight physical at Fort Riley. The flight surgeon falsely reported that Davis had a history of epilepsy. U.S. Army Air Corps Headquarters flew Davis to Maxwell Field in Montgomery, Alabama, for another physical. Davis passed without trouble. Davis suspected that flight surgeons routinely found "deficiencies" when examining African-American candidates.

Davis took flight-training classes with other cadets.

Davis began his pilot training. It included classroom courses such as science, engineering, aeronautics, and navigation. He also took flying lessons. He learned how to take off, maneuver, and land the aircraft. Before a cadet was allowed to fly solo, he flew with an instructor who gave instructions from the backseat. Out of a class of 13, Davis was one of five who moved from primary onto basic training at TAAF. He learned how to make forced landings, flips, and rolls. He also concentrated on military flying and received instruction in night flying.

During Davis's training, the Japanese bombed the U.S. Navy base at Pearl Harbor in Hawaii on December 7, 1941. The United States declared war the next day. The United States joined the Allies—Great Britain, France, and Russia—in a war against Japan, Germany, and Italy. The United States was officially a part of World War II.

On March 7, 1942, Davis received his wings at a ceremony at the TAAF base. He and his classmates would be the first pilots assigned to the Ninety-ninth Fighter Squadron, an all-African-American fighter unit. But Davis's military career was just beginning. He received two sets of orders in mid-May. The first set promoted him to major. The

Roosevelt's Civilian Pilot Training Program

In 1938, President Franklin D. Roosevelt began a pilot-training program to create a reserve of trained civilian fliers in anticipation of being drawn into the European conflict. It was called the Civilian Pilot Training Program. Only after much political pressure was the program opened to African Americans. Tuskegee Institute participated in the program. It allowed the institute to train pilots using government funding. In 1941, First Lady Eleanor Roosevelt visited Tuskegee Institute and met many of the people in the pilot-training program. She even took a ride in an airplane with Chief Flight Instructor Charles Anderson, affectionately known as "Chief."

A Select Few

When Benjamin O. Davis Jr. was chosen to lead the U.S. Army Air Forces' all-African-American flying unit, the Ninety-ninth Fighter Squadron, he was one of only two African-American officers serving with combat units in the army. The other was his father, Benjamin O. Davis Sr.

second promoted him to lieutenant colonel. Shortly thereafter, Davis received orders designating him commander of the Ninety-ninth Fighter Squadron. The Ninety-ninth soon filled with successive classes of trained pilots. At full strength, it was ready for combat—and ready to fight for the warring country. Many people, including Davis, wondered how the newly formed U.S. Army Air Forces would utilize its first African-American flying unit. ⌐

Instructors at Tuskegee Institute taught Davis how to fly.

Chapter 5

Davis often gave direction to other pilots, such as Lieutenant Charles W. Dryden, left.

THE TUSKEGEE AIRMEN IN WWII

In April 1943, the Ninety-ninth Fighter Squadron finally received its deployment orders. The 400 members of the squadron boarded the ship *Mariposa*, docked in Brooklyn, New York. The men of the Ninety-ninth were not the only troops on board the *Mariposa*. There was a total of 4,000 troops on the ship. Of those men, approximately 15 percent were African American. But Benjamin O. Davis Jr. was given a key administrative position. He was appointed troop commander, making him a senior officer among all the troops on the ship. This was a stark and welcome difference to the segregation and racism that Davis and the squadron had faced before.

The Ninety-ninth then traveled to a training base in Oued N'ja. The base was in the middle of French Morocco in North Africa. There, a dirt strip had been cleared for the squadron to use. The men had to build their own latrines, sleep on the ground, and create a base in Oued N'ja. New P-40 Warhawks arrived for the Ninety-ninth. The pilots were pleased about these planes, as their training had been on older aircraft. The pilots spent their time training for combat. They engaged in combat exercises with the Twenty-seventh Fighter Group stationed at a U.S. base nearby. Davis enjoyed seeing North Africa. He specifically appreciated a reprieve from the racism in the United States.

The Ninety-ninth moved from French Morocco to a combat base at Fardjouna, Tunisia. The

squadron would be attached to the Thirty-third
Fighter Group commanded by Colonel William
Momyer. Davis reported to Colonel Momyer, and
he was received in an official manner. Pilots at
Fardjouna were assigned dive-bombing missions.
They also escorted bombers and ship convoys,
protecting them from enemy attacks.

IN COMBAT

In June 1943, Davis and the Ninety-ninth went
into combat. Their mission was to strafe—to fly low
and fire machine guns at targets on the ground, such
as bridges and truck convoys. The pilots also would
drop bombs on targets identified by intelligence
officers. The mission took place on Pantelleria, an
Italian island in the Mediterranean Sea. For the first
time, the pilots faced enemy aircraft.

Combat flying was much different and more
nerve-racking than flying in friendly skies. Pilots
had to work collectively, fly in formation, and
keep a careful watch for enemy flyers. Many of the
German aircraft were faster and could fly higher
than the Ninety-ninth's P-40s. The enemy used the
advantage to make high-speed passes and choose the
place and time of engagement.

The Ninety-ninth Fighter Squadron destroyed parts of Pantelleria during a combat mission.

Although Davis and his men gained confidence from experience, they also experienced heartache. On July 2, Davis led a 12-plane escort of B-25s in southwest Sicily, a large island off the coast of mainland Italy. During this mission, the Ninety-ninth shot down an enemy aircraft and damaged another. However, the Ninety-ninth also lost pilots. Davis later likened the loss of a pilot to the death of a family member.

Pantelleria soon surrendered, followed by two other islands near Sicily, Lampedusa and Linosa. The Americans set up an air base on the southern coast of Sicily. With the Allies now targeting Sicily, the Ninety-ninth played a part in escorting bombers to Sicily, dive-bombing enemy supply warehouses, and destroying enemy communications. The enemy was driven out of Sicily in August 1943.

A NEGATIVE REPORT

Davis had been pleased with the performance of the Ninety-ninth. He was certain that the squadron would continue to develop and improve. But not every officer in the Thirty-third Fighter Group agreed with him. A negative report written by Colonel Momyer made it to the McCloy Committee

In Response to "Unofficial Reports"

Davis was greatly angered by a *Time* magazine article entitled "Experiment Proved?" that was published in the magazine's Monday, September 20, 1943, edition. The article questioned the combat performance of the Ninety-ninth Fighter Squadron. Additionally, the article cited unofficial reports about the future role of the Ninety-ninth in the war. Information regarding the role of a fighter squadron was classified. This kind of leak was particularly upsetting to Davis.

Agatha Davis was angry as well. She wrote a letter to *Time* magazine in response to the article. In her letter, Agatha chastised the magazine for citing such unofficial reports. She argued that *Time* magazine's article might give a false impression and create negative opinion about the Ninety-ninth. *Time* printed Agatha's letter. Benjamin Davis also responded to the negative article. When asked about discrepancies between the article and Davis's assessments of the Ninety-ninth, the Army Air Forces Headquarters stated that it stood by Davis's report.

of the U.S. War Department. The McCloy
Committee made policy regarding employment of
African-American troops in combat. Despite the
performance of the Ninety-ninth, the U.S. Army
Air Forces and the U.S. War Department still had
doubts about African-American pilots. Momyer's
report criticized the work of the Ninety-ninth
and its pilots' abilities. The report recommended
that all African-American squadrons be assigned
noncombatant duties.

Momyer's negative report created misgivings
about the Tuskegee experiment and put the entire
future of the African-American airmen in jeopardy.
Davis was furious. He felt that the report and its
criticisms were unwarranted and unreasonable.
He decided to fight back. He called a press
conference at the Pentagon, which houses the U.S.
Department of Defense, and gave his account of the
Ninety-ninth's performance.

In October 1943, Davis was ordered back to the
Pentagon to report to the McCloy Committee. Davis
testified to the committee, challenging the negative
report and giving a fuller picture of the training
and experience of the Ninety-ninth. He stated that
Momyer's report did not reflect the improvements

made by the Ninety-ninth after gaining experience in combat. Nor did the report recognize the stamina of the pilots who had functioned for two months without replacement personnel.

Davis's tactics with the McCloy Committee were strategic. He did not bring up racism, even though that was the obvious reason for the negative report. Instead, Davis presented facts in a quiet, reasoned manner that he hoped would yield positive results. During his testimony, Davis also raised the idea of training African-American and white soldiers together.

Davis's testimony did not lay all doubts to rest, but it did help motivate the army to examine the issue further. The army ordered a study called "Operations of the 99th Fighter Squadron Compared with Other P-40 Squadrons in the Mediterranean Theatre of Operations." The study would compare the Ninety-ninth to other fighter units in regard to combat readiness, missions, enemy losses, and casualties of war. The study covered the period from July 1943 through February 1944. Meanwhile, Davis would have his hands full working with the 332nd Fighter Group.

Men from the Ninety-ninth Fighter Squadron

Pilots listen to a mission briefing in Italy in September 1944.

CONFLICT ON THE
GROUND AND IN THE SKY

In 1943, Benjamin O. Davis Jr. had more to worry about than the study on the Ninety-ninth's performance. He had a new assignment. In October, Davis reported to command the 332nd Fighter Group at Selfridge

Field near Detroit, Michigan. He was walking into a difficult situation. The base had experienced problems with discrimination and racism in the past. The 332nd had several support units and three squadrons of Tuskegee airmen, the 100th, the 301st, and the 302nd. Except for its white commander, Colonel Robert S. Selway Jr., and his white training personnel, the 332nd was entirely an African-American fighting group.

Before Davis's arrival, base commander Colonel William Boyd had denied African-American officers entry to the officers' club. This was in direct violation of Army Regulation 210-10. It stated, in part, that officers' clubs and mess halls had to extend the right of full membership to all officers on duty at the base. The base commander's actions had nearly caused a riot.

When Davis arrived, he realized that tensions were high and noted a lack of discipline. He also observed a lack of experience and maturity in the ranks. Davis worked closely with his

"No officer clubs, messes, or similar organization of officers will be permitted to occupy any part of any public building . . . unless such club, mess, or other organization extends to all officers on the post the right to full membership."[1]
—*Army Regulation 210-10, published in 1940*

commanders to offer support. He needed to get his men ready for combat. Still, racial issues persisted and segregation remained a problem.

In the winter of 1944, Davis returned to Italy with the 332nd Fighter Group. Davis was frustrated by the assignment, believing that the 332nd was not seeing real combat. He did not share his opinion, though, and performed his duties without reservation. The 332nd handled coastal patrol missions as convoy escorts, provided harbor protection, reconnaissance (information-gathering missions), and strafing. During this time, Davis learned that he had been recommended for the Legion of Merit for his service with the Ninety-ninth. He was proud of the squadron and viewed the recommendation as a positive acknowledgment of the Ninety-ninth's success in combat.

An Opportunity to Help

Effective air warfare in World War II was critical to victory. Warfare depended on major bombing campaigns of military targets and major cities. Bombers were larger aircraft that moved more slowly than fighters. They flew in formation. The bombers used escort fighters to turn away enemy aircraft

A Fifteenth Air Force bomber is destroyed over Germany. The Fifteenth bombers needed protection to prevent such losses.

that were defending the cities or military targets. In the spring of 1944, the Fifteenth Air Force needed fighter escorts to protect bombers that destroyed German supply lines and factory centers in France and Germany. General Ira Eaker of the Fifteenth thought that the 332nd could help.

Davis saw escorting the bombers of the Fifteenth as a great opportunity for his pilots. White pilots did not want the mission, because they would not engage in combat or receive credit for personal victories. But Davis recognized the mission's importance in the war effort. The 332nd could play a more offensive role and engage the enemy. His pilots were not as upbeat about the assignment—they wanted to chase down fighters, not escort bombers. Davis made clear to his pilots the importance of the mission. Additionally, he stated that any pilot who left a bomber unprotected would be grounded, accused of breaking military law, and subject to court-martial.

GAINING RESPECT

In April 1944, the results of the "Operation of the 99th Fighter Squadron Compared with Other P-40 Squadrons in the Mediterranean Theatre of Operations" study were in. The study found that the Ninety-ninth was a "superb tactical fighter unit."[2] It concluded that no significant differences existed between the performances of the Ninety-ninth and other P-40 squadrons in the Mediterranean. The abilities of the Ninety-ninth would no longer be questioned.

Visit from Joe Louis

Joe Louis was a African-American boxer from Detroit, Michigan. He became the heavyweight boxing champion of the world after defeating Jim Braddock in 1937. Louis was a celebrity, a national hero, and a great inspiration to all African Americans.

During World War II, Louis took a year off from boxing to serve his country in the military. Staff Sergeant Joe Louis visited the 332nd when they were based in Italy. Many of the men of the 332nd had photos taken with the champ during his visit.

More good news arrived. In May 1944, Davis
was promoted to colonel and the 332nd met up
with General Eaker's Fifteenth Air Force. The
Ninety-ninth Fighter Squadron joined the 332nd
Fighter Group. Colonel Davis led the 332nd as its
pilots flew their escort mission with the Fifteenth
Air Force in June 1944. As formation leader,
Davis was responsible for takeoff and joining up
with the bombers. Under the 332nd's protection,
the bombers attacked factories and oil refineries
in German-occupied territories, among other
targets. On the way to a target during a mission over
Munich, Germany, enemy airplanes attacked. In the
ensuing air battle, five enemy planes were shot down,
but not a single Fifteenth Air Force bomber was lost.
The 332nd pilots served the Fifteenth well. Upon
returning to base, the bomber commanders had a
message for their escorts: "Your formation flying
and escort is the best we have ever seen."[3]

RECOGNITION FOR THE 332ND

Thereafter, the 332nd distinguished itself in
combat. And after the ground crews painted the
tails of their planes red, the 332nd earned a new
nickname—the Red Tail Squadron. The Red Tails

scored numerous aerial victories and shot down many enemy fighters. Morale soared as they received praise.

The 332nd received a visit from General Eaker, General Nathan Twining, General Dean Strother, and Davis's father, Benjamin O. Davis Sr. on September 10, 1945. Four pilots, including Davis Jr., received the Distinguished Flying Cross. Davis received it for his leadership on the mission over Munich in June 1944. His medal was pinned on him by his father.

Italy

Italy is an independent nation in southern Europe. In the north, Italy has the high peaks of the Alps. In the south, the country juts into the Mediterranean Sea. Italy is known for its painters, sculptors, ancient buildings, and picturesque scenery. Many tourists visit Italy to learn from its history, enjoy its fine food, and explore historic ruins.

During World War II, Italy joined with Germany against the Allies. At the time, the fascist dictator Benito Mussolini ruled Italy. Italy entered the war after Germany had almost completely conquered France. Thereafter, Mussolini invaded southern France. Mussolini's armies faced many defeats. Eventually, foreign armies invaded Italy. Germany helped Mussolini fight off the Allied troops for a time in Northern Italy, but they too were overcome. Mussolini fled toward Switzerland. However, he was captured and killed by antifascist Italians.

After the war, in 1946, the Italian people voted to make their country a republic. The republic adopted a new constitution and held elections. In 1947, Italy signed a peace treaty and the Allies withdrew their troops from the nation.

But the successes did not end there. The airmen who trained at Tuskegee engaged in combat with the best the German Air Force had to offer. Later in the war, the 332nd faced some of the first German jet fighters. On one mission, three enemy jets were destroyed, and the 332nd suffered only one loss. During this undertaking, the 332nd had completed the full 1,600-mile (2,575-km) mission by flying without replacements for relief. This mission earned the 332nd the Distinguished Unit Citation. The honor recognized the outstanding skill and determination of the pilots as well as the great technical skill and devotion of the ground crews.

Germany had surrendered on May 7, 1945. The war in Europe was over, though Japan still held out against the Allies. During a crucial phase of World War II, the 332nd had not only distinguished itself in

Promoting African Americans in the Military

African-American war correspondents visited the 332nd. They played an important role in keeping the United States informed about the activities of African Americans in the military. The African-American press also played an important role in reporting about Tuskegee Army Air Field, Selfridge, and other bases where African-American personnel were stationed. African-American publishers were able to exert pressure to help advance the role of African Americans in the Army Air Forces.

combat, but it had never lost a single bomber to an enemy fighter. By the end of the war, the 332nd had flown more than 1,500 missions, destroyed hundreds of enemy aircraft, and been awarded 150 Distinguished Flying Crosses. This valor and effort were not without cost. Sixty-six pilots of the 332nd did not make it home. In describing his pilots, Davis wrote:

> *Despite treatment that would have demoralized men of lesser strength and character, they persisted through humiliations and dangers to earn the respect of their fellows and others who learned of their accomplishments.*[4]

*A Distinguished Flying Cross medal, like the one
Davis received for his leadership*

An officers' club in Fort Myer, Virginia

COMMAND AND
SEGREGATION

fter Victory in Europe (V–E) Day, on May 8, 1945, the 332nd Fighter Group was deactivated. But the war was not over yet. Japan continued to fight. Benjamin O. Davis Jr. had orders to assume command of the 447th

Bombardment Group at Godman Field, Kentucky. He was the first American of color to be placed in charge of an entire military installation.

Godman would be a challenging command for Davis. The 447th had been activated for 17 months, yet it still had not achieved combat readiness. Davis knew that the main problem was racial conflict. The African-American trainees and the white supervisors clashed often, and African-American officers faced discrimination in gaining promotion. In addition, the unit had been forced to move frequently because of problems with local white communities and other issues. This constantly interrupted training. Morale at the 447th was terrible.

Colonel Robert S. Selway Jr., a white West Point graduate, had been in command of the 447th before Davis. Selway refused to recognize the racial problems, and his actions served only to exacerbate them. Selway was backed by Major General Hunter, who believed in segregation. Once again, the issue of the use of the officers' club was a contributing factor to the conflicts. At Godman, Selway sought to maintain segregated officers' clubs by having whites join the all-white club at nearby Fort Knox, leaving the club at Godman all African American.

The African-American officers viewed this as a violation of Army Regulation 210-10, which stated that all officers were allowed entrance to such clubs. The African-American officers organized a protest and attempted to enter a restricted club at Freeman Field, Indiana. They were refused entrance, and those who got through were arrested. Later, after receiving legal advice, Selway had all of these men released except for three who had used force in the protest. Selway then tried to make all personnel sign a regulation agreeing to the segregation of the officers' clubs. Approximately 100 African-American officers refused to sign the regulation and were arrested.

These imprisoned officers managed to get word of their situation to their families and the outside world. The National Association for the Advancement of Colored People (NAACP) protested the arrest of the men. The National Urban League, a civil rights group, asked Congress to investigate. A number of senators became involved. The McCloy Committee reviewed the situation and issued a report stating that Selway had authority to arrest the African-American officers involved, but his other actions conflicted with army regulations.

In the end, only the three officers who had used force were charged. The case against two of the officers collapsed. The final officer was found guilty of shoving a superior and received a fine.

CHANGE OF COMMAND

Meanwhile, Davis was assigned to make the troops ready for combat. He believed that Selway's and Hunter's racist actions had interfered with preparing the troops in the past. Davis flew to Godman on June 21, 1945, with General Eaker, who was now the deputy commander of the Army Air Forces. Truman Gibson and his father, both members of the McCloy Committee, traveled with him as well.

General Eaker attended the change of command ceremony, reflecting the Army Air Forces' confidence in Davis. Agatha traveled from Washington DC to attend

National Association for the Advancement of Colored People

The NAACP was founded in 1909. Throughout its history, the NAACP has fought segregation, racism, and discrimination. Among its many efforts, the organization helped with civil rights legislation and fought in the court system to end segregation. The NAACP continues to fight for equal rights and against racial discrimination.

the ceremony, too. General Eaker praised Davis's combat record and informed the troops that Davis would select his own staff and supervise the combat training. General Eaker also informed the troops that the 447th would become a composite group with two bomber squadrons and one fighter squadron. Selway and his staff were relieved of their command.

The 447th Squadron

Davis worked hard preparing the 447th for combat. African-American officers received the promotions they had been denied and morale improved at Godman. Still, Davis had to face the racist attitudes of the commanding general of Fort Knox. As Selway and his white personnel prepared to vacate their quarters, Davis requested housing for his men and their families. His request was denied solely because of race. In a letter to the First Air Force Headquarters, the post commander at Fort Knox complained that African Americans should not be allowed housing at the honored, historical fort because their presence might offend the white general officer residents.

Davis and his men wound up being housed in crowded quarters in barrack buildings at Godman.

The buildings were unpleasant and conditions were appalling. The barracks were adjacent to barracks occupied by prisoners of war being held at Fort Knox. Davis thought it was a disgraceful way to treat combat veterans. He would never forget this shameful treatment of war veterans and their families by officers of the U.S. Army.

Through it all, Davis maintained his focus on preparing his men for combat. Then, in August 1945, the United States dropped atomic bombs on the Japanese cities of Hiroshima and Nagasaki. Japan surrendered to the United States and its Allies on September 2, 1945. The 447th would

Roosevelt's War Objectives

In the State of the Union message delivered to Congress on January 6, 1941, U.S. President Franklin D. Roosevelt outlined four basic freedoms essential to every individual. The first was the freedom of speech and expression. The second was the freedom of every person to worship in his or her own way. The third was the freedom from want, and the fourth was the freedom from fear.

President Roosevelt also highlighted his commitment to national defense and to supporting the security of the United States. He expressed the need to increase armament production, urging Congress to provide funds to do so. The president intended to send ships, planes, tanks, and artillery to U.S. allies fighting in defense of freedom.

He also called for U.S. citizens to make sacrifices, including paying more taxes. The taxes were to pay for the increased defense spending by the government. President Roosevelt sought a world order where countries were free and cooperated in a civilized society. He also expressed support for human rights everywhere.

not see combat against the Japanese. World War II
was over.

THE NIPPERT REPORT

After the war ended, the U.S. War Department
reviewed reports of the African-American
units in combat. Lieutenant Colonel Louis
Nippert summarized these reports and issued his
recommendations. Submitted on September 17,
1945, the Nippert Report cited significant flaws
with the performance of African-American
troops in combat. It criticized African-American
officers as well. The report also stated that most
of these deficiencies were considered the result
of poor education and poor training as well as a
lack of technical work experience in noncombat
life. The Nippert Report recommended that
military segregation continue. Still, the report also
recommended that all Air Force specialties be open
to African Americans to pursue.

The U.S. War Department created a board of
generals to study the issue of African Americans
in the military. Led by Lieutenant General Alvan
Gillem, the Gillem board reviewed the Nippert
Report and interviewed many officers and civilian

leaders. Some witnesses opposed integration. Air Force commander Carl Spaatz testified that African Americans were low achievers. General Ira Eaker, who had received help from the 332nd for bomber escort missions, testified against integration. William Hastie, the former civilian aide to the secretary of war, was one of several witnesses who called for the immediate integration of the military. The white Tuskegee Air Field commander Colonel Noel Parrish also supported integration by calling for equal treatment of all citizens.

On April 27, 1946, the Gillem board recommended limited racial integration. This meant, in effect, that segregation would continue. However, many people, including Davis, still strongly advocated for complete integration.

At this point, the future of African Americans in the military

"Whether we dislike or like Negroes and whether they like or dislike us, under the Constitution of the United States, which we are sworn to uphold, they are citizens of the United States, having the same rights and privileges of other citizens and entitled to the same applications and protection of the laws."[1]

—*Tuskegee Air Field commander Colonel Noel Parrish*

remained unclear. During the war, President Roosevelt had told the citizens of the United States that they were fighting for freedom. Now that the war was over, what would that mean to the African Americans in the U.S. military? What opportunities would Davis have? —

Commander Carl Spaatz was against desegregation in the Army Air Forces and testified that African Americans were low achievers.

Many African-American pilots were trained at Tuskegee Army Air Field until it closed in 1946.

THE CHANGING MILITARY

With the end of the war, Benjamin O. Davis Jr.'s responsibilities eased. He was now dealing with peacetime duties and training. For example, the 447th needed a new home. Davis helped find a new base for his men. Air Force

Headquarters moved the 447th to Lockbourne, near Columbus, Ohio, in March 1946.

Initially, local citizens objected to the move—they did not want African-American neighbors. But, over time, tensions with the local population in Columbus eased and relations improved. Davis was glad to be out of the South and away from the Jim Crow segregation laws.

The 447th's move to Lockbourne was a major step in the struggle for equal rights. African Americans were going to manage an Army Air Forces' base without the direct regulation of white officers. This was a first for the United States. In 1946, the Tuskegee Army Air Field (TAAF) was closed. Tuskegee pilots who wanted to stay in the air force were reassigned to Lockbourne Air Force Base. Training of African-American pilots would now take place at Randolph Field, Texas.

In many ways, life at Lockbourne was a great improvement over Godman, especially in the area

Lockbourne Officers' Wives Club

When Davis arrived at Lockbourne Air Force Base, he was impressed with its appearance. However, there was a lot to be done. The barracks needed to be made into family housing for the families of the men who worked on the base. In the meantime, families lived all over the Columbus area. Agatha Davis and other wives at Lockbourne helped to create a community among the families connected to the base. They formed the Lockbourne Officers' Wives Club. The club created a day care for children on the base. It also raised money for social events and charities such as the Red Cross.

Planes flying over the administration building at Randolph Field, Texas, where training for African-American pilots took place

of housing. Davis and Agatha lived in a former farmhouse with a large garden. Still, segregation within the air force remained a problem, and it led to frustrating personnel issues for Davis. Many trained, experienced African-American men left the service, leaving Davis to fill key positions. However, filling the empty posts proved difficult. Qualified white pilots could not serve under an

African-American commander. Similarly, if the 447th had too many African-American pilots of the same specialty, they could not be assigned to a white unit to better utilize their skills. In 1947, the 447th became the 332nd Fighter Wing. As a result, many crewmen who specialized in bomber planes were left without an assignment. These men could not be reassigned even though white bomber groups were in need of their skills.

Trip to Liberia

In June 1947, Davis joined his father as an aide on a trip to Liberia, a country in western Africa. Davis Sr. was designated a special representative to Liberia. Father and son traveled on the aircraft carrier USS *Palau* for Liberia's 100th anniversary celebration. Davis was impressed with what he saw on the ship. On February 28, 1946, the navy had issued a directive on segregation. The directive read:

> *Effective immediately, all restrictions governing the types of assignments for which Negro naval personnel are eligible are lifted. Henceforth, they shall be eligible for all types of assignments in all ratings in all activities and all ships in the naval service.* [1]

On the *Palau*, Davis was amazed by how well the African-American and white personnel had been integrated. His experience in the Army Air Forces was that segregation was officially and unofficially set. In contrast, the sailors and marines he met on the ship were assigned based on abilities, not race. Davis noted that integration worked well in both on-duty and off-duty situations. Davis knew that the navy was not completely integrated. Most African Americans in the navy still did not hold combat positions. Still, what Davis saw on the *Palau* gave him hope for more integration within the Army Air Forces.

EXECUTIVE ORDER 9981

On September 18, 1947, after Davis's return from Liberia, the Army Air Forces became a separate branch of the military service—the U.S. Air Force. Around that time, Lieutenant General Idwal Edwards commissioned a study of racial issues inside the U.S. Air Force. The study was intended to improve military efficiency and the use of manpower. Edwards thought segregation wasted the potential of many African Americans.

Many within the U.S. Air Force still feared integration and worried that it would have disastrous results. Despite this opposition, the U.S. Air Force moved forward to integrate African Americans.

Then, on July 26, 1948, President Harry S. Truman signed Executive Order 9981 calling for the armed forces to provide equal treatment and opportunity for African-American servicemen. The president also appointed a committee to make sure integration was properly implemented. Finally all U.S. Air Force jobs and training were open to African Americans. Before they could be reassigned, African-American personnel needed to be screened by a review board to assess their skills. Davis was named president of a screening board at Lockbourne.

Davis believed in the high standards and performance of the Lockbourne personnel. He was

---

Executive Order 9981

Signed at the White House on July 26, 1948, Executive Order 9981 stated:

It is hereby declared to be the policy of the President that there shall be equality of treatment and opportunity for all persons in the armed services without regard to race, color, religion or national origin. This policy shall be put into effect as rapidly as possible, having due regard to the time required to effectuate any necessary changes without impairing efficiency or morale.[2]

Proponents of segregation argued for "separate but equal" treatment for African Americans. But the president's order was not about "separate but equal" accommodations and opportunities. It outlawed all kinds of segregation in the armed forces.

not surprised when integration took on a life of its own in the U.S. Air Force. In May 1949, the 332nd was inactivated, as its personnel had been integrated worldwide. By the end of December 1950, 95 percent of the African-American airmen in the U.S. Air Force served in integrated units. Lockbourne Air Force Base was closed.

Some African-American personnel had reservations about their new assignments, but Davis's men adjusted well. Some attributed their success to their former commander. Davis had been strict, fair, and held consistently high standards for his men. The men who had formerly belonged to the 332nd appreciated the quality of their training and soon earned the respect of their white peers.

As the U.S. Air Force continued to integrate successfully, many previous fears and objections were laid to rest. Clearly, the excellent performance of the African-American fighter units and the success of Lockbourne Air Force Base helped influence the movement's success. Davis's leadership and unwavering determination had been integral to the success of integration in the U.S. Air Force.

Benjamin O. Davis, Jr.

On July 26, 1948, President Harry S. Truman
signed Executive Order 9981.

Two fighter jets return to their carrier after an air strike during the Korean War.

INTERNATIONAL POSTS

Segregation had always hung like a cloud over Davis and Agatha when they lived on military bases, even at the more comfortable Lockbourne. As they left Lockbourne in August 1949, they knew that legally sanctioned segregation would no longer haunt them in the military. Yet they were realistic. An executive order did not erase prejudice and racial hatred in the military, nor did it change civilian life in the rest of the country. Davis and Agatha moved to Maxwell Air Force Base in Alabama, where Davis would be a student at the Air War College. Davis viewed this opportunity as recognition that he was being prepared for promotion. He was determined to succeed in the next phase of his career.

Davis graduated from Air War College on June 16, 1950. He received orders to report to the Pentagon as a staff-planning officer within the Directorate of Operations, U.S. Air Force. This meant a move to racially segregated Washington DC. Davis and Agatha had trouble finding decent housing in the African-American neighborhoods.

The Korean War

At about this time, North Korea invaded South Korea. At first, Davis's work at the Pentagon did not focus on the Korean War. But soon he was made chief of the Fighter Branch. He was also given several other responsibilities. The most important responsibility given to Davis at this time was to supervise the fighter program of the U.S. Air Force worldwide. This meant ensuring that all fighter units achieved the highest level of combat capabilities.

Air power was an important aspect of the Korean War and made work at the Pentagon extremely challenging for Davis. He worked long days, weekends, and sometimes nights handling the critical role that fighters played in the war. Davis was involved in important developments regarding the fighters, such as improved in-flight refueling to allow fighters to fly longer ranges. Davis took a trip to Tokyo, Japan, and Korea to visit Far East Air Force (FEAF) Headquarters and Korea-based fighter units. He wrote a report containing his assessments and recommendations for the fighter units.

During Davis's tour of duty at the Pentagon, he requested and received approval to create the Thunderbirds. The Thunderbirds are the official air demonstration team of the U.S. Air Force. The team creates interest in training and recruiting aviation cadets, demonstrates flying precision and proficiency, and promotes public interest in the U.S. Air Force. Davis's office was responsible for the success of this precision flying operation.

Also during this time, the U.S. Air Force was transitioning to jet fighters. So, senior officers needed to become familiar with jet operations and flying. In 1953, Davis had his first introduction to jet aircraft. He attended a course on jet aviation at Craig Air Force Base.

In 1953, Davis was to be transferred to FEAF in Korea. He looked forward to the challenges, but not to the prospect of being so far from Agatha. He would be stationed in Korea for one year, and Agatha was not allowed to join him. Before Davis left, he trained at Nellis Air Force Base in Las Vegas, Nevada. His training was challenging and exciting. But the Korean War ended in July 1953, when Davis was still training in Las Vegas. He continued his training and prepared for a new assignment.

In November 1953, Davis assumed duties as commander of the Fifty-

The Thunderbirds

On May 25, 1953, the U.S. Air Force's official air demonstration team, the Thunderbirds, was activated. At its inception, the demonstration team was based at Luke Air Force Base in Arizona. The name *Thunderbirds* was inspired by Native American culture and folklore of the Southwest. The first demonstration team was made up of 7 officers and 22 enlisted men. The first aircraft selected for the demonstration team was the F-84G Thunderjet. The original demonstration consisted of a series of formation aerobatic maneuvers that lasted about 15 minutes.

first Fighter Interceptor Wing, FEAF. It was an integrated tactical unit made up largely of whites in Suwon, Korea. Active conflicts had ended in the country, yet the possibility of renewed fighting was high. Davis had to make sure the Fifty-first Fighter Interceptor Wing was ready to fly combat missions with no notice.

Racism in a Classroom

As a light-skinned African American, Agatha Davis's experience of racism was somewhat different from other African Americans. One time, while her husband was stationed at the Pentagon, Agatha Davis took painting classes at the YWCA in Washington DC. During her study, the YWCA decided to integrate. Soon after, Agatha's painting teacher called Agatha at home. The teacher informed Agatha that she thought integration was terrible. She refused to teach African Americans. In protest, the teacher had decided to hold her classes in her home, and she invited Agatha to attend.

Agatha informed her teacher that she had been teaching an African American all along. The teacher was shocked to learn that Agatha was African American. She informed Agatha that she would have to ask permission from the other students for Agatha to be able to attend the classes. Agatha recognized the woman's racist attitude. She refused to take another lesson from the teacher.

AROUND THE WORLD

Soon Davis received a new assignment that would lead him to another Asian country. He was to be the director of operations and training at FEAF Headquarters in Japan. His mission was to develop and maintain combat readiness. Agatha joined him in

Japan. Davis loved Tokyo, feeling free from segregation in this international environment. Davis and Agatha felt more welcome than they had ever felt in the military before. They explored Japanese culture and made many friends.

Tokyo

Tokyo is the capital city of Japan. Its name translates as "eastern capital." The city is situated on low plains and lies adjacent to upland hills. It is a center for industry, culture, commerce, tourism, and finance in Japan.

In October 1954, President Dwight D. Eisenhower nominated Davis for promotion to brigadier general. He received his first star. Later that year, Davis returned to the Pentagon to discuss FEAF's role in responding to any threat to Taiwan, which was an independent island off the coast of China. China had vowed to take the island but President Eisenhower and the U.S. Congress had made a commitment to the defense of Taiwan. Davis was ordered to be vice commander of the Thirteenth Air Force and commander of the Air Task Force Provisional Thirteen. His new station would be Taipei, Taiwan.

When Davis took command, China had strategic advantages. Davis helped contribute to Taiwan's air defense. Under Davis's command, the Air Task Force Provisional Thirteen achieved combat readiness. The assignment in Taiwan helped accelerate Davis's career. Once again, he earned a reputation as an effective commander. Davis also established friendships in Taiwan that transcended race and nationality.

In May 1957, Davis was assigned to duty in Ramstein, Germany. There, he would be chief of staff of the Twelfth Air Force, United States Air Force in Europe (USAFE). The Twelfth Air Force held joint responsibility for the defense of territory in France and Germany. Later, Davis undertook responsibilities as deputy chief of staff for operations at USAFE headquarters in Germany. Davis and Agatha made numerous friends and enjoyed traveling to different European countries. Then, in 1959, Davis was awarded a second star. This made him the first African-American officer to achieve the rank of major general.

Davis and Agatha finally returned to the United States in July 1961. They moved to Bolling Air Force Base. Davis was assigned to serve at U.S. Air Force headquarters as the director of manpower and organization. The return to Washington DC was an adjustment after the freer, more open societies that Davis and Agatha had experienced abroad. On August 28, 1963, Dr. Martin Luther King Jr.

Benjamin O. Davis Jr. gives a briefing in 1958.

delivered his "I have a dream" speech at the Lincoln
Memorial. Davis and Agatha strongly supported civil
rights and followed the civil rights movement closely.

In 1965, Davis was assigned as assistant deputy
chief of staff at the Pentagon. He had held that
post for only a few weeks when he was promoted

to lieutenant general and received assignment as chief of staff for the United Nations Command and U.S. Forces in Korea. In that position, he developed social skills that would prove to be an enormous help in both his and Agatha's lives. ⁓

United Nations

The United Nations (UN) is an international organization of nations that was created on October 24, 1945, by 51 countries. On that date, the UN Charter was ratified by a majority of signatories. They included, among others, the United States, China, France, the Soviet Union, and the United Kingdom. The UN had 51 member states in 1945. In 2009, the UN had 192 member states.

The UN headquarters is in New York City, but the organization has offices around the world. It focuses on maintaining peace and security worldwide and upholding respect for international law. The UN also aims to promote friendly relations among countries and peaceful resolutions to international issues.

Benjamin O. Davis Jr. in his Pentagon office in April 1965

*Airplanes are guarded at Clark Air Base
in the Republic of the Philippines.*

FROM MILITARY TO
CIVILIAN LIFE

*I*n 1967, Benjamin O. Davis Jr. assumed
command of the Thirteenth Air Force at
Clark Air Base in the Republic of the Philippines.
He reported to the commander of the Seventh Air
Force with headquarters in Saigon, which oversaw the

air war in Vietnam. Since 1964, the United States had been trying to prevent North Vietnam from taking over South Vietnam and uniting the country under a communist government.

Clark Air Base provided support to operations in Vietnam. It did not participate in actual combat. One of the major challenges Davis faced was trying to improve the relationship between Filipinos and U.S. citizens. Many Filipinos held great distrust and even hatred for U.S. citizens. Davis and his wife used the diplomatic skills they had learned in their recent years abroad to improve relations with their new host country.

During this time, Davis and Agatha were disappointed to learn that President Lyndon B. Johnson would not seek reelection. They viewed Johnson as a positive force in improving the stature of the United States around the world. They also believed he had improved the lives of African Americans. Under his leadership, laws that legalized segregation and denied African Americans the right to vote were deemed unconstitutional. Even more disturbing news reached Davis and Agatha in the Philippines. Dr. Martin Luther King Jr. had been assassinated on April 4, 1968.

In August 1968, Davis was assigned as deputy commander in chief, U.S. Strike Command, with headquarters at MacDill Air Force Base, Florida.

Lyndon B. Johnson

Lyndon B. Johnson served in Congress for almost a quarter century. In 1960, he was elected vice president of the United States. On November 22, 1963, President John F. Kennedy was assassinated, and Johnson became the thirty-sixth president of the United States. The swearing-in ceremony took place aboard the presidential air force jet shortly after Kennedy died. In 1964, Johnson was elected president of the United States.

Johnson used his experience in the legislature to push for civil rights laws and education laws. On July 2, 1964, Johnson signed the Civil Rights Act of 1964. This legislation guaranteed equal job opportunities for all. It opened public accommodations, such as hotels and restaurants, to African Americans.

In 1965, Johnson urged Congress to pass the Voting Rights Act to ensure voting rights for African Americans. Federal examiners were authorized to register qualified voters and end practices that prevented African Americans from voting. The Civil Rights Act of 1968 banned racial discrimination in the sale or rental of houses and apartments. Additionally, the legislation provided federal protection to civil rights workers. On March 31, 1968, Johnson announced that he would not seek reelection for a second term.

After having spent three years living abroad, Davis and Agatha had misgivings about returning to the South. Still, they understood that military life involved reassignment.

Both Davis and Agatha felt welcome at Strike Command. Strike Command had been organized in the 1960s and operated directly under the Joint Chiefs of Staff. This group maintained operational command over all assigned combat-ready ground forces and air forces in the United States. Strike Command was responsible for uniting assigned army units and air force tactical units into joint forces that could quickly react under a single command.

On Veterans Day 1969, Davis spoke at the dedication ceremony of a new school in Compton, California: the Lt. General Benjamin O. Davis Jr. Junior High School. Shortly after, Davis met up with his fighter and bomber pilot comrades from World War II for a reunion. Davis had served his country well and his determination had helped bring about many important changes in the military. After 37 years of service, Davis retired from the military on February 1, 1970.

After Military Retirement

Soon after retiring from the military, Davis accepted a position under Cleveland Mayor Carl Stokes

Joint Chiefs of Staff

The Joint Chiefs of Staff (JCS) is the top military advisory group in the United States. It advises the president of the United States, the secretary of defense, and the National Security Council. The JCS includes the chiefs of staff of the U.S. Army and U.S. Air Force, the chief of naval operations, and the commandant of the Marine Corps. The chairman is appointed by the president with the approval of the Senate. The chairman presides at meetings and outranks all other officers. The chairman also makes recommendations to the president. On military committees of international organizations, the JCS represents the United States.

as director of public safety. Stokes was the first African-American mayor of a major U.S. city. At the time, Cleveland was plagued by crime as well as racial strife. Davis's job entailed ensuring the public safety through the police department, the fire department, the office of traffic management, and the dog pound. But Davis found that he did not work well with Stokes's administration. Frustrated with urban politics, Davis resigned as director of public safety.

Hijacking

Hijacking is the unlawful commandeering of a land vehicle, aircraft, or other form of transport while it is in transit. Hijackings can be financially motivated, with the hijackers demanding huge ransom payments in exchange for the safety and release of the passengers and crew. Hijackings can also be politically motivated. For example, hijackers might demand the release of prisoners in exchange for the safety and release of the passengers and crew or use a hijacked plane as a weapon of destruction.

In June 1970, President Nixon appointed Davis to the Campus Unrest Commission, a unit designed to prevent on-campus violence. Many student-led antiwar protests in response to the Vietnam War were occurring on campuses across the nation. Among other things, the commission was charged with identifying what caused campus violence.

On September 21, 1970, Davis accepted the position of director of civil aviation security in the U.S. Department of Transportation. This newly created position was

*Benjamin O. Davis Jr. speaks at a news conference
as director of civil aviation security.*

designed to address the issue of commercial aircraft
hijackings, also referred to as skyjackings. Skyjacking
had become a problem and a danger to citizens
during this era. Davis's role was to improve security
on the ground and in the air to end all forms of
hijackings. He focused on improving airport and
aircraft security by making airports and airlines safe
from criminals, saboteurs, and terrorists. Trained
and armed, federal sky marshals were placed onboard

aircraft to act as deterrents. Hijackings significantly decreased.

Davis went on to become assistant secretary of transportation for safety and consumer affairs in 1971. During his tenure, he lobbied for the speed limit on highways to be lowered to 55 miles (88 km) per hour to decrease fatal accidents. Davis worked at the department until he retired in 1975. Upon retiring he received the department's highest award, the Gold Medal for Achievement.

THE LAST YEARS

Davis spent his retirement years engaged in a variety of activities. This included speaking at programs that educated people about the role of African Americans in the military and in aviation. In 1978, President Jimmy Carter appointed Davis to the Battle Monuments Commission, the same commission on which Davis's father had served. The Battle Monuments Commission commemorated the contributions of the armed services personnel who had given their lives for their country. In 1991, Davis published his autobiography. Then, on December 9, 1998, President Bill Clinton awarded Davis a fourth star, advancing him to general.

Agatha passed away on March 10, 2002. Only a few months later, on July 4, Davis died at the age of 89. He had been battling Alzheimer's disease. Davis's coffin was draped with an American flag, and he was buried with full military honors at Arlington National Cemetery in Virginia. Hundreds of people attended his funeral. They included a group of Tuskegee airmen, who bid a final farewell to their comrade.

Mourners praised Davis as an intrepid leader, a pioneering military officer who broke color barriers and destroyed racial myths. Many of the mourners' comments reflected the sentiments of Virginia Governor L. Douglas Wilder, who once stated:

Arlington National Cemetery

Arlington National Cemetery is a national burial ground in Arlington County, Virginia. It was established in 1864 on the Potomac River directly opposite Washington DC. The cemetery serves as burial ground for casualties of war. Arlington is the final resting place of many prominent soldiers and civilians including President John F. Kennedy, Jacqueline Kennedy Onassis, Supreme Court Justice Thurgood Marshall, President William Howard Taft, Chief Justice of the U.S. Supreme Court Earl Warren, astronauts, and prominent explorers.

Throughout his achievements, General Davis has exemplified the West Point motto, "Duty, Honor, and Country." But more important, his life has reflected the social changes that have taken place in the United States over the last 50 years. Through the strength of his commitment to his principles and goals, he has been an inspiration to all those who have followed and served under him, and he will continue to be so for as long as there is a United States military. Indeed, Benjamin O. Davis's life is testament that we are living to see the moral reconstruction of this country.[1]

On December 9, 1998, Benjamin O. Davis Jr. was awarded his fourth star.

TIMELINE

1912	1932	1936
Benjamin O. Davis Jr. is born in Washington DC on December 18.	Davis enters West Point on July 1.	Davis graduates from West Point ranking thirty-fifth in a class of 276.

1942	1942	1942–1945
In March, Davis completes the flying course at Tuskegee Army Air Field.	Davis is promoted to lieutenant colonel and commander of the Ninety-ninth Fighter Squadron.	Davis is stationed in North Africa, the United States, Italy, and Europe.

1936	1938	1941
Davis marries Agatha Scott on June 20.	Davis is appointed professor of military science at Tuskegee Institute.	Davis joins the Army Air Corps as part of the "Tuskegee experiment."

1945	1948	1950
On June 21, Davis becomes the first African American to command an air force base on U.S. soil.	On July 26, President Truman issues Executive Order 9981 providing for integration of the armed forces.	Davis graduates from Air War College at Maxwell Air Force Base on June 16.

TIMELINE

1954	1959	1965
President Eisenhower nominates Davis for promotion to brigadier general on October 27.	Davis becomes the first African-American officer to be made major general.	President Johnson promotes Davis to the rank of lieutenant general in April.

1978	1991	1998
Davis becomes a member of the Battle Monuments Commission.	Davis publishes his autobiography.	President Clinton awards Davis his fourth star and promotes him to the rank of general.

Benjamin O. Davis, Jr.

1970

Davis retires from the U.S. Air Force on February 1.

1970

Davis takes a job as director of civil aviation security in September.

1971–1975

Davis serves as assistant secretary of transportation for safety and consumer affairs.

2002

Agatha Davis dies on March 10.

2002

Benjamin O. Davis Jr. dies of complications from Alzheimer's disease on July 4.

Essential Facts

Date of Birth

December 18, 1912

Place of Birth

Washington DC

Date of Death

July 4, 2002

Parents

Benjamin O. Davis Sr. and Elnora Dickerson Davis

Education

Western Reserve University, Cleveland, Ohio; University of Chicago, Chicago, Illinois; United States Military Academy at West Point, New York; Air War College, Maxwell Air Force Base, Alabama

Marriage

Agatha Scott (June 20, 1936)

Children

None

Career Highlights

In 1941, Davis joined the U.S. Army Air Corps as part of the "Tuskegee experiment." In March 1942, Davis won his wings as one of five African-American officers to complete the flying course at Tuskegee Army Air Field. Davis was named commander of the first African-American air unit, the Ninety-ninth Fighter Squadron, in 1942. He led the Ninety-ninth to many successes during World War II. On June 21, 1945, Davis became the first African American to command an air force base on U.S. soil when he took command of Godman Field in Kentucky. In 1959, Davis became the first African-American officer to be made major general.

Societal Contribution

Benjamin O. Davis Jr. broke color barriers and destroyed racial myths. His efforts helped end segregation in the armed forces. Living a life of high standards, duty, honor, and integrity, Davis became a role model and a hero.

Conflicts

Benjamin O. Davis Jr. served in the United States armed forces during World War II, the Korean War, and the Vietnam War. Throughout his life, Davis faced racism and discrimination and yet succeeded as he rose through the ranks in the armed forces.

Quote

"Despite treatment that would have demoralized men of lesser strength and character, they persisted through humiliations and dangers to earn the respect of their fellows and others who learned of their accomplishments."—*Benjamin O. Davis Jr., describing the pioneering African-American pilots with whom he flew in World War II*

ADDITIONAL RESOURCES

SELECT BIBLIOGRAPHY

Davis, Benjamin O. *Benjamin O. Davis, Jr., American.* Washington DC: Smithsonian Institution Press, 1991.

Dryden, Charles W. *A-TRAIN: Memoirs of a Tuskegee Airman.* Tuscaloosa, AL: University of Alabama Press, 1997.

Fletcher, Marvin. *America's First Black General: Benjamin O. Davis, Sr. 1880–1970.* Lawrence, KS: University Press of Kansas, 1989.

Harris, Jacqueline. *The Tuskegee Airmen: Black Heroes of World War II.* Minneapolis, MN: Dillon Press, 1996.

FURTHER READING

Clinton, Catherine. *The Black Soldier: 1492 to the Present.* Boston, MA: Houghton Mifflin Books for Children, 2000.

Fleischman, John. *Black and White Airmen: Their True History.* Boston, MA: Houghton Mifflin Books for Children, 2007.

Jones, Steven L. *The Red Tails: World War II's Tuskegee Airmen.* Logan, IA: Perfection Learning, 2001.

Web Links

To learn more about Benjamin O. Davis Jr. visit ABDO Publishing Company online at **www.abdopublishing.com**. Web sites about Benjamin O. Davis Jr. are featured on our Book Links page. These links are routinely monitored and updated to provide the most current information available.

Places to Visit

Arlington National Cemetery
Arlington, VA 22211
703-607-8000
www.arlingtoncemetery.org
More than 300,000 people are buried at this national cemetery.

National Museum of the U.S. Air Force
1100 Spaatz Street, Wright-Patterson AFB, OH 45433
937-255-3286
www.nationalmuseum.af.mil
This museum hosts many military aviation artifacts. Exhibits at the museum display historical aircraft, equipment, and weapons.

Tuskegee Airmen National Historic Site
1616 Chappie James Avenue, Tuskegee, AL 36083
334-724-0922
www.nps.gov/tuai
This historic site commemorates the airmen who served their country during World War II with distinction in spite of segregation and racial discrimination.

GLOSSARY

aeronautics
 The science dealing with the operation of aircraft.

armament
 Weapons.

aviator
 The operator, or pilot, of an airplane.

barnstorm
 To pilot one's airplane through rural districts staging exhibition stunts or to perform sightseeing flights with passengers.

bomber
 An aircraft that drops bombs.

cadet
 A person who is formally training to become a member of the armed forces.

combat-ready
 Engaged in or prepared for military operations.

command
 The authority to be in charge of and direct a military unit.

discrimination
 Prejudiced action or treatment often on racial, ethnic, or religious grounds.

exacerbate
 To make a bad situation worse.

intrepid
> Fearless and unrelenting toward a goal.

jet
> An aircraft powered by jet engines.

Jim Crow laws
> The laws that enforced racial segregation in the South from the late nineteenth century into the 1950s.

Ku Klux Klan
> An organization that tried to promote white supremacy through intimidation and violence.

segregation
> The separation or isolation of a race, class, or ethnic group by enforced or voluntary residence in a restricted area, by barriers to social interaction, by separate education facilities, or by other discriminatory means.

squadron
> An operational air force group made up of two or more groups of aircraft and the people needed to fly them.

stationed
> To be assigned to a particular area.

strafe
> To continuously attack with bombs or machine guns from a low-flying aircraft.

tactical unit
> A military, air force, or naval group that functions in combat as a single unit.

Source Notes

Chapter 1. Flying High in the Wind
None.

Chapter 2. A Child of the Military
None.

Chapter 3. Silence Is Deafening
None.

Chapter 4. The Tuskegee Experiment
1. Benjamin O. Davis. *Benjamin O. Davis, Jr., American.* Washington, DC: Smithsonian Institution Press, 1991. 57.

Chapter 5. The Tuskegee Airmen in WWII
None.

Chapter 6. Conflict on the Ground and in the Sky
1. Benjamin O. Davis. *Benjamin O. Davis, Jr., American.* Washington, DC: Smithsonian Institution Press, 1991. 94.
2. Jacqueline Harris. *The Tuskegee Airmen: Black Heroes of World War II.* Minneapolis, MN: Dillon Press, 1996. 64.
3. Ibid. 71.
4. Benjamin O. Davis. *Benjamin O. Davis, Jr., American.* Washington, DC: Smithsonian Institution Press, 1991. 94.

Chapter 7. Command and Segregation
1. Jacqueline Harris. *The Tuskegee Airmen: Black Heroes of World War II.* Minneapolis, MN: Dillon Press, 1996. 117.

Source Notes Continued

Chapter 8. The Changing Military
1. Benjamin O. Davis. *Benjamin O. Davis, Jr., American.* Washington,
DC: Smithsonian Institution Press, 1991. 154.
2. "Executive Order 9981." *Harry S. Truman Library and Museum.* 9 Apr.
2009 <http://www.trumanlibrary.org/9981a.htm>.

Chapter 9. International Posts
None.

Chapter 10. From Military to Civilian Life
1. Benjamin O. Davis. *Benjamin O. Davis, Jr., American.* Washington,
DC: Smithsonian Institution Press, 1991. Foreword x.

INDEX

INDEX CONTINUED

ABOUT THE AUTHOR

Sari Earl is an attorney. After winning first place in a writing competition, she began a full-time writing career. In addition to published novels of adult fiction, Earl has written articles and young adult books. She writes fiction and nonfiction and enjoys the challenge of both. Her books have been published in countries around the world. Earl lives with her family in Atlanta, Georgia.

PHOTO CREDITS